This book is on loan from
Library Services for Schools

County Council

what we do

Chef

JAMES NIXON

PHOTOGRAPHY BY BOBBY HUMPHREY

FRANKLIN WATTS
LONDON•SYDNEY

First published in 2012 by Franklin Watts

Franklin Watts
338 Euston Road
London NW1 3BH

Franklin Watts Australia
Level 17/207 Kent Street
Sydney, NSW 2000

Planning and production by
Discovery Books Limited
Editor: James Nixon
Design: sprout.uk.com limited
Commissioned photography: Bobby Humphrey

Dewey number: 641.5'023

ISBN: 978 1 4451 0889 6

Printed in China

Franklin Watts is a division of Hachette
Children's Books, an Hachette UK company.

www.hachette.co.uk

Acknowledgements: Shutterstock Images:
pp. 2 (Monkey Business Images),
15 bottom-left (Spilman), 22 (Tonis Valing),
23 bottom (Joe Seer).

The author, packager and publisher would like
to thank Art's Café Bar & Restaurant, Leeds,
for their help and participation in this book.

what we do

CONTENTS

4 I AM A CHEF

6 GAINING EXPERIENCE

8 THE HEAD CHEF

10 CREATING A MENU

12 BUYING INGREDIENTS

14 USING EQUIPMENT

16 COOKING TECHNIQUES

18 UNDER PRESSURE

20 HEALTH AND SAFETY

22 GETTING ON

24 GLOSSARY

24 INDEX

Words in **bold** appear in the glossary on page 24.

I AM A CHEF

My name is Phil. I work as a **sous chef** in the kitchen of a restaurant. My job is to prepare and cook food that customers order from the menu.

I work as part of a team to get the meals served on time. If I am cooking the main courses, other chefs will prepare starters and make desserts. Chefs need to know all about the ingredients that make up different kinds of meals and learn lots of different cooking techniques.

► *This is the outside of the restaurant where I work.*

Kitchens are busy, hot, noisy and exciting places. The shifts can be long and tiring. But if you are passionate about creating good food, then this job might be for you.

▲Chefs need to have lots of energy, as they spend most of the time on their feet.

▼Learning how to create new dishes is an exciting part of being a chef.

My favourite part of the job is experimenting with new dishes. I am always learning and working on new things. The worst part of the job is the long hours. Three days a week I work from 9am until 10pm! Sometimes I work six days a week.

KEY SKILLS

ABILITY TO WORK UNDER PRESSURE – When service gets really busy you need to work quickly and calmly, and not get flustered.

GAINING EXPERIENCE

As a sous chef I work under the head chef. I run the kitchen when he is away. In bigger kitchens there are section chefs who handle a particular type of work, such as sauces or **pastry**. To work your way to the top you need to gain experience in all parts of the kitchen.

This is Mourad (below), our **commis chef**. He is training towards becoming a chef by learning the skills of cooking on the job. Direct work experience is the best way to learn.

▲ *Here, I am teaching Mourad how to cook chips in the fryer.*

KEY SKILLS

TEAMWORK AND COMMUNICATION – The different sections of the kitchen must work well together to make sure the food is ready on time.

◄ *Although Mourad is a trainee, the food he prepares will be served to paying customers, so he cannot make mistakes.*

▲ *Mourad does basic food preparation, such as peeling potatoes.*

▼ *Salads do not have to be cooked but they must be presented perfectly.*

Commis chefs start off by learning basic skills, such as preparing vegetables. They often serve salads and cold starters as they cannot be over- or undercooked. Trainees will spend a number of years gaining a range of skills in different sections. Then they are ready for a **promotion**.

A trainee chef can start work without any qualifications. However if you are looking for a position, you will find it easier if you have good GCSEs, especially in Catering, Maths and English. Kitchen experience is useful – many commis chefs are promoted from **kitchen porters**.

THE HEAD CHEF

This is Jamie (right), our head chef. He is in charge of the whole kitchen. It is Jamie's job to make sure that every dish is produced to the highest quality.

Head chefs need to be good communicators. They **supervise** the cooking at every stage. Jamie sometimes teaches me a new dish on the menu. He tells me how much flavouring to add to the food and checks that I cook it for the right amount of time. Then he will test the food for taste (below).

▲ *Kitchens can be hectic places, so Jamie is loud, clear and forceful with his instructions.*

The head chef must be well organised. His or her team will be working on lots of different dishes at the same time, but the customers can't be kept waiting for long. Jamie is constantly in communication with us, asking questions, such as 'Have you got this ready? What's next?' All of his staff must understand what is going on and the jobs that they have to do.

▶ *Jamie makes sure that the food is presented and served properly.*

▼ *As head chef, Jamie is usually 'on the pass'. This is the part of the kitchen where the food is passed to the waiter or waitress.*

LEADERSHIP – The quality of the food depends on the way head chefs manage their staff.

CREATING A MENU

The head chef also has the task of producing a menu that will be popular with the customers. The restaurant has to make a **profit,** too. Chefs work out the prices for the menu, based on the cost of the ingredients.

Jamie reviews the menu every six weeks. The changes he makes to the menu depend on what is selling well. The dishes on the menu often reflect the season. We try to use ingredients that grow at that time of year.

▼ *Jamie calculates the cost of each dish on the menu.*

art's VALENTINES MENU

STARTERS

Sweet potato & chestnut ravioli, tomato & roast garlic fondue with sage & caper butter, sweet potato crisps (V)

Smoked haddock & crab Scotch egg, asparagus mayonnaise, pea shoots & parsley oil

Chicken liver parfait, seared fois grois, vanilla roast plums & toasted brioche

MAINS

Roast rack of lamb & pressed shoulder, parsnip puree, spring cabbage & cider jus

Pea mint & feta spring rolls with baby pear & watercress salad (V)

Asian spiced monkfish & salt & pepper king prawns with coriander, soy & ginger noodles

DESSERTS

Assiette of desserts to share – lemon & vanilla panna cotta, iced raspberry lollipops, warm fudge brownie & raspberry coulis

PRICES

£29.95 per person
Price includes a glass of sparkling wine on arrival

WWW.ARTSCAFEBAR.CO.UK

Chefs make sure there is plenty of choice for people with different tastes. There is usually a **vegetarian** option, for example, and both fish and meat.

Top chefs are fascinated with food and flavours, and the different ways food can be served. Jamie does lots of research and experimentation when he is inventing dishes. He will look at other restaurants' menus, search the Internet, and use old cookbooks to get ideas. He often likes to take old-fashioned recipes and give them a modern twist. Each week he puts a new 'chef's special' on the menu.

KEY SKILLS

CREATIVITY – Imagination is needed to produce quality food and keep the menu varied and interesting.

▲ *Jamie puts the finishing touch to his latest chef's special – fried squid on top of a pork belly stir fry.*

11

BUYING INGREDIENTS

A chef must make sure that the kitchen is stocked with all the ingredients needed for the menu. To source the best ingredients chefs need a good understanding of all their recipes.

▼ *Sometimes Jamie pops to the market to find an ingredient.*

Each morning I check to see if any foods have run out or are running low. Then I make phone calls to order in any new supplies. We have separate suppliers for meat, fish, vegetables, and dry goods, such as spices and rice.

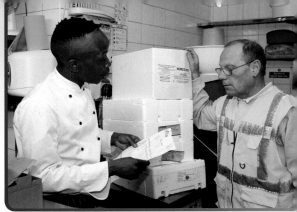

When the food deliveries arrive (above) I check that everything is there and that there is no damage, such as bruising (left). The food then has to be stored at the correct temperature. Meat and fish goes in the freezer. We put fruit and vegetables in a special **chiller room** at the back of the kitchen (below).

Chefs also have to be careful not to order too much food. Throwing away food is a waste of money. Experienced chefs can predict how many customers there will be. They are aware that factors, such as the weather and the time of year, can make a difference.

USING EQUIPMENT

Chefs start their career by doing the most basic jobs and gradually learn more skills. There are a variety of kitchen **utensils** and appliances that chefs use.

Knife skills are essential techniques for a chef. There are different knives for foods, such as bread, fish and vegetables. When cutting, it is vital that you keep your fingers out of the way (above). Here, I use my knuckles as a guard and keep the tips of my fingers tucked in.

KEY SKILLS

ABILITY TO LEARN QUICKLY – As a trainee chef, you have to learn techniques and put them into practice straight away.

With this knife (left), I grip the handle tightly and place the point of the knife on the board. Then I slice the vegetable with the back of the blade. Hours of practice give chefs the necessary speed and **precision** when cutting.

When I **fillet** a piece of chicken or fish I know exactly where to find all the fat and bones to cut out (left). A chef's work should always be neat and tidy, and every dish should be presented identically.

TOOLS OF THE TRADE

Blenders, mixers, microwaves and fryers are just some of the appliances in the kitchen. This is Jamie changing the settings on the oven. Depending on the type of food being cooked, he turns a dial to change the amount the food gets **roasted** or **steamed**.

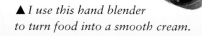

▲ *I use this hand blender to turn food into a smooth cream.*

► *Here, I am getting to grips with the electric mixer.*

COOKING TECHNIQUES

Chefs gradually master more complicated techniques by spending time in different areas of the kitchen. When it comes to cooking food there are a variety of methods that chefs learn.

Meat has to be cooked perfectly – if it is under- or overcooked it will not taste right. You can braise meat, by cooking it slowly in liquid in a pot. Stewing food in a pot is a similar technique – I keep stirring a stew, so it does not burn at the bottom (right).

▲ *For some dishes I flame-grill or flame-fry meat, to give it a smoky flavour.*

The trick with any kind of cooking is to know when something is done. Here (above), I am testing fish with my fingers. If the fish springs back when I gently touch it, then it is cooked. Sometimes we poach fish – this cooks it in a pan of hot liquid, such as milk.

Pastry and breadwork are areas that require advanced skills. When rolling pastry I have to be very precise. If you overwork the pastry it will fall apart. Here (right), Jamie is **kneading** bread properly, so it will rise in the oven. Some chefs specialise in one particular area, such as making desserts, and become real experts.

KEY SKILLS

ATTENTION TO DETAIL – Cooking food is a delicate job and even the slightest error may mean you have to throw food away and start again.

UNDER PRESSURE

The atmosphere in a kitchen can be frantic. When the restaurant is full and orders are arriving all the time, chefs are under pressure to keep up with the pace and produce great meals really quickly.

▲ *I work quickly under pressure.*

Not only do I have to be fast, but I also have to make sure that every single dish is neatly presented and cooked to the same high standard.

▲ *The orders are pinned up in a long line to remind us what needs doing.*

When lots of orders arrive at once, you have to stay calm and keep a clear head. Even in an organised kitchen things will go wrong. Food can be burned, plates or pans can be dropped. It is important that you do not panic and perform your best to sort out the situation quickly.

Rushing around on your feet in a hot, steamy kitchen for long periods of time is incredibly tiring. I find it exciting and lots of fun, but the job is not suited to everyone.

KEY SKILLS

STAMINA – You need to keep going even if you are exhausted.

SPEED – There is no time to waste in a kitchen.

MULTI-TASKING – You must cope with several tasks at once.

HEALTH AND SAFETY

A busy kitchen can be very dangerous. It is a hot place full of stoves, ovens and sharp tools. Chefs must know how to act safely to avoid scars, burns and serious accidents.

To handle hot dishes and pans we use heat-proof towels or gloves (right). If there is a spillage on the floor I mop it up immediately and stand a wet-sign up to warn others.

Food preparation must be carried out in a clean environment. If an **Environmental Health Practitioner** turns up and sees a dirty kitchen, the restaurant could be shut down.

▼ *After each service, we clean the surfaces with hot water and* **sanitiser.** *We also mop and sweep the floors, including the store rooms.*

PERSONAL HYGIENE – It is important to show a high standard of cleanliness.

I tend to wipe down dirty services as I go along, and I scrub the floor every hour or so. Our uniform is white so that dirty stains show up and can be cleaned. If you have long hair you have to wear a chef's hat.

▲ *Hands must always be washed between tasks.*

TOOLS OF THE TRADE

The chopping boards we use for food preparation are colour coded. This is so certain types of food do not get **contaminated** with other foods. If raw meat found its way on to a customer's salad it could make them very ill. Some customers may be **intolerant** to a particular type of food, such as nuts or dairy products, so it is important that foods do not get mixed up.

COLOUR CODED CUTTING BOARDS
eliminate the risk of bacterial cross contamination during food preparation

RAW MEAT

RAW FISH

COOKED MEAT

SALAD & FRUIT

VEGETABLES

BAKERY & DAIRY

GETTING ON

As a trainee chef you will be expected to gain some certificates at college while you work. If you cannot find an **apprenticeship,** attending a course at college is a great way to enter the industry.

■ The main qualifications for **aspiring** chefs are the *Level 1 and 2 Diplomas in Professional Cookery* awarded by City and Guilds. The college will offer you work experience placements as you learn. *Level 1* covers the basic elements of cookery. *Level 2* covers further

ingredients and recipes. Once you have gained these qualifications employers will know that you have the skills for the job.

■ There are lots of job opportunities for chefs. Chefs are needed anywhere that food is prepared, from restaurants and hotels, to schools, hospitals and prisons. Professional catering companies serve large numbers of people, such as a television crew on set.

▼ *Catering companies employ large numbers of staff.*

▲ *Head chef Jamie has appeared on the TV show,* Masterchef: The Professionals.

■ A *Level 3 Diploma* develops your skills further and qualifies you to be a head chef. Head chefs reach their position by rising through the ranks and will probably have worked for a number of different employers. Experienced chefs can start up their own restaurant. Running a business brings extra responsibilities, but can be very **lucrative**.

▶ *Celebrity chef and multi-millionaire Gordon Ramsay.*

Some top chefs become famous celebrities, such as Jamie Oliver and Gordon Ramsay. Ramsay owns a number of restaurants around the world. The first restaurant he opened, in London, is one of the few in the world to hold three **Michelin stars**, an award that chefs dream of.

KEY SKILLS

PASSION – You should have a passion for food and the different dishes that can be created.

GLOSSARY INDEX

apprenticeship A trainee position where you learn the skills of the job as you work.

aspiring Describes someone who wants to achieve something.

budget The amount of money that is available to spend.

chiller room A cold room for storing food a few degrees above freezing point.

commis chef A junior chef, who is just starting his or her career.

contaminate Mix up with something that should not be added.

Environmental Health Practitioner An inspector who checks that the food prepared in restaurants is safe to eat.

fillet To remove the bones from food, such as fish or chicken.

hygiene The practice of keeping yourself and your surroundings clean.

intolerant Unable to eat something for medical reasons.

kitchen porter A person employed to wash dishes and carry out other basic tasks in a kitchen.

knead Press and squeeze into a dough with the hands.

lucrative Producing a lot of profit.

Michelin star An award given to restaurants where the quality of the food is judged to be outstanding.

pastry A mixture of flour, fat and water used to cover baked dishes, such as pies.

precision If you show precision you are extremely accurate in your work.

profit A sum of money that you gain when you sell something for more than you bought it for.

promotion If you are promoted you are given a more important and higher paid job at work.

roast To cook using dry heat in an oven.

sanitiser A disinfectant used for killing germs.

sous chef The assistant to the head chef. Sous means 'under' in French.

steam To cook using hot steam from boiling water.

supervise To direct and check what someone is doing to make sure that they do it correctly.

utensils Tools for practical use.

vegetarian A person who does not eat meat and sometimes other animal products.

appliances 14, 15

braising 16
bread 14, 17

catering companies 22
celebrities 23
chopping boards 21
cleaning 20, 21
commis chefs 6, 7
customers 4, 6, 9, 10, 13

desserts 4, 17
dishes 5, 8, 9, 10, 11, 15, 18, 23

equipment 14–15

fish 11, 13, 14, 15, 17
flavours 8, 11
food preparation 7, 20, 21
frying 6, 16

head chefs 6, 8–9, 23
hygiene 21

ingredients 4, 10, 12–13

knives 14

main courses 4
meat 11, 13, 16, 21
menus 4, 8, 10–11
mixers 15

orders 18, 19
ovens 15, 20

pastry 6, 17
poaching 17

qualifications 7, 22, 23

Ramsay, Gordon 23
recipes 11, 12
restaurants 4, 18, 20, 22, 23
roasting 15

safety 20–21
sauces 6
shifts 5
sous chefs 4, 6
starters 4, 7
steaming 15
stewing 16
supplies 13

trainees 6, 7, 17, 22

uniform 21

vegetables 7, 13, 14